Mortality and Glory

Raffi Basmadjian autobiography Part 1

Road and Unrest

Raffi Basmadjian autobiography Part 2 (In the making)

Early life

I was born may 13 1983 in Beirut mdawar Lebanon I have 2 sets of parents my giving birth mother and her husband and government s of Bulgaria Russian federation Soviet federation with blood and Syria with blood where my parents did because of bad relationships with their maronite s including tragedy.

Family

I come from son of Fatima s harout with grandparents baptized Fatima from Syria Armenian orthodox dirouhy and husband Lebanon Armenian catholic Guiragos. Also my mother Fatima from Lebanon Armenian orthodox and parents Armenian orthodox of millionaire status who are relative of House of lords royal and deputy governor of Lebanon central bank. All Cilician s I am a Latin high cilician because of my mother father relation with former Ottoman back then domestic ally to USSR Bulgaria where gave me my high cilician status and my father side 3rd generation about 100 years Latin from Syria sent to Lebanon grandmother Dirouhy.

School

I enter 3 years of age agbu private school garmirian which is school for privilege background primarily and attend there enjoying as I remember aroma of nature from this ny headquarters western Armenian school which reminds me of jabal lbnan aroma of blend of status rain and smell s from the garden s outside the school till this day the smell has big impact on me United with its Lebanon NY and Armenian curriculum.

Social life

I rememlrem2 sets of social life one school the other same organization club section where I was scout since 4 or 5 years old and enjoy outdoor indoor scout experience including car wash day on school property and general scouting on Sunday morning s till the center was built and changed to Saturday afternoon s the other social life is school recess where we enjoy playing PC games in elementary school and extracurricular activities where I was a chess player playing against cherish friend mainly. I was not famous but had deep friendships.

First crush

I was first grade and I had crush on my Armenian teacher and spent art time fixing my homework and was so improved she yelled don't have your mother do your homework I showed her that was me was impressed one day she gave me a flower I hid it for months then my mother threw it away I was disappointed another time I knew were going to Armenian religious evening I within pararmeter search her and not find was disappointed . Other than this I had crush on 2 Armenian females of my age and both unsuccessful though both regret during teenage years.

Lebanon war

When I was born Lebanon was at Civil war that ended in 1990 I remember my father under sniper s bringing teacher and student s to their home I remember taking shelter in 2nd floor Sunni Muslim family neighbor who after the war because of philange threat left to UAE to live like muslims one of the things I remember about this unique impression left family was my mother cook pizza after them eating would ask my mother if there was pork in the pizza.

Sharkieh

Was hate zone and as I remember I remember this 2 family report s the bombing started we must go home etc. And second it Finish early would be culturally correct to assume that the target died. I also remember roads closed with walking and taxis leaving the war zone. I remember coming back home and removing the white blankets off the sofas I remember my father saying they came.

Zahle

My father has told me has lent 10000 usd to his sister to buy apartment in Damascus so has the key of their apartment in zahle and I live my childhood in zahle from war times my parents use to go to Beirut and sometimes return because of bombing while we live in zahle so I know zahle slot during the war 1 year I went Armenian church school in zahle is snow having city that does not snow a lot but is cold so mountain face clothing body clothing is worn that year more than snow freezing is the main attribute of the city while living there my aunt use to take us to brdawni we use to go to al wading a lot and of course zahle had 1 busy street that money having kids want the market place I know zahle a lot and I remember as a small place of doesn't change.

Damascus

Damascus is big with teenage students in military uniform yellow taxi with meters and international taxis yellow again Syrian that park too close to each other Damascus is big my cousin knew the store that sold illegal during hafez Assad time American goods which we use to buy had to call the dollar green because was illegal and intelligence strong and everyone afraid they also use to put sheet and sell on the street the country is famous for people market hummus tasty so is the people food the country is famous for corn where the condition people make by intelligence similar and the water of the corn tastes the same at every buyer and is not exactly home water though with pride. When war in Lebanon we frequently used to go to Damascus and in Lebanon my father use to call the Syrian army the cleaners. We use to eat where high profile eat. My aunt husband use to being Syria arf for dinner and my father ask when Syria will leave Lebanon anger the arf and say never this was one of my father contributes I remember growing up.

Teenager

I turn out to be sexy teenager with long hair and pale skin I was going tekeyan school my both 8 and 9th grade and was first I was famous with money and was like a doll for bourj hammoud ramgavar school with poor people background.

Friends and females

As teenager I was a class and friends and women were a team even teachers gave me special attention and a team socialite from intermediate school according to age . I succeed the bravest by half grade and not go technical school and go secondary school.

High school

I attend agbu private school s hovagimian Tarouhy secondary school 11th grade I do humanities digit number students mostly female and one other Male and I do my 12th grade sociology and economics where the Lebanon court s judges I catch jaundice judges that schoolmates are parasites and in me them transfer more spoken Lebanon court section and regularly according to ministry of education and late traffic Hariri I am putten by background and merit to suny empire state.

Moral

One of the moral is I acquire the concept the fetish of the taught and expand on the subject this is by understanding and not learning hard I succeed I listen to teacher explain in class and give back instead of learning at home.

Fame

I become one of the most famous student of the secondary school with women wanting and watching me the female security teacher groping me the Male security teacher picking me for cigarettes having and division s gossiping about me.

Social life

I enter playing ti nu for ABBA I discontinue 12th grade after football injury reaching orange belt important not professionally defend oneself. I play football for the secondary school and with crush es go to discos. My parents were strict once I escape school with classmates waiting to socialize I wear picture t shirt internationally to be sent home not go home spend the day calling sick classmates.

Intelligence and growing up

My mother being from sharkieh tells me not to cooperate with Lebanon but I since driving I use the internal security force regularly and am accepted.

Mimosa executive

Syrian Lebanese army come and force shoot gun in his brain and the investigation finds that he playing with the gun was wrongfully shot the son of the executive all remember s is my father name harout factory of catholic maronite mix background was giving old equipment s free to Syria for Syrian wealth creation my father also once told me that he would have driven Porsche and not care about me.

Maronite neighbors

On mariam day I am watching at home polsat alone about 23 years old I decide to masterbate on women and from the balcony I do the family with grown son all maronite come I'm home alone and from their face they want to teach me lesson I say I'm alone I get scared they say will come back later so when my family comes I go intentfully to my grandfather building in Rabieh the next day I come and my mother tells me what I have done the Syrian Lebanon military ousts them from their home and come shortly after Syria leaves the Lebanon military again ousts them out not to come again.

Tekeyan principal

A millionaire Armenian principal for party protection has told me he doesn't need the money is there for organization during my intermediate school years and new realize period the millionaire eye gets him killed by Syria and Lebanon military and the party brings professional from agbu to continue as school and me student there.

Raffi Rzian

A commoner in secondary school that start Armenian Lebanon treason in collaboration with grown ups including my uncle against me the Syrian and Lebanon military gives him cancer and dies within months was the first treason movement from rmeil and was a rude person believe in above god for horror s will be rewarded for example use to want a sandwich tells what want s inside and not simple what not and gets angry he says 5 normal ingredient s and does not want 1 which is not including instead of not tomato which was the ingredient not including and cancer from sandwiches is what killed him.

Maral losing her womb

I was light blooded by the government when I visited the hospital the government took future fertility away.

Inaash bank closed purchase by sgbl

Maral deputy branch manager relation with family closed the bank for me with direct grand assault against me cause when she got married with boss godfather and kicked from in laws apartment my grandfather spoke next to my bed about her and gorgodian. Freemason leader said inaash owner visit his village.

Government protections

Government also provides protection from active violence during civil war and post war because of nature of maronite s Lebanon provide act of God and government protection which growing up includes to following

Soviet aerospace

When I was child I had over me Soviet aerospace defend me wherever I went and fighting whether safely tucked at home watching the skies or back of my father car going to zahle them looking like child dream following from the sky protecting.

Bomb falls neighbor empty apartment

Gather at my grandfather apartment in Beirut mar Michael during Civil war my father and grandfather passionately speaking politics I don't remember when time to leave home near the door missile bombing and explosion at that time the apartment was empty it falls in the master bedroom on the bed we go and see the ceiling hole was the government maronite s where trying to exterminate the family and the government by act of God diverts with message to neighbor empty master bedroom.

Sniper bullet hits the wall between me and my grandfather

During the war another episode my grandfather standing at our home back balcony I am inside playing a maronite sniper trying to kill me from forensic I did later as qualified the government diverts the bullet which hits the balcony wall at child height leaving 10 cm square whole with grandfather the government diverts with message to that status maronite s want to assassin me.

17years old maronite shoot s the football to my head

My father decided when I was early ten ish years to put me colony de vacance at maronite s sages to learn Arabic maronite s use armeni terminology official ly and that summer we go to Bulgaria for 1 more brother the Bulgaria guide explains black sea how Turks attacked and they were afraid thus name black sea then the fear went away when came from those 7 days to colony 17 years old maronite with most power shoots the football direct hit my head to assassin the government protects slav style like balloon.

University

Rafiq Hariri part of direction puts me suny empire state part of official Lebanon relations my Arabic was so weak I apply in English baccalaureate material such as sociology and economics and from 10th grade the superior command on American culture was evident so much I have a fiction essay about armageddon still kept the grading for essay in philosophy and language Hollywood from transcripts against the teacher explain but affected in 2500 instead of new laws of continue the dying nation sends to survivor the laws which is the Armageddon with subliminal message to know to fix. School message was to live to write and philosophy is from Greek writing will diminish the memory. The director of 2 traditional Armenian parliamentary school puts me humanities. And I have curb to positive like 1 percent USA faith of Lebanon. Suny empire state was created to educate hippies in 1970s and is by military difficult role. This secret is heart of Nations.

Early stage

I continue my early stage like high school with no learning detail the second year I pursuit learning with over achieving shift from my money background traditional to be Frank with all my achievements I would rather open a retail clothing from my mother rent put aside 30000 usd in bourj hammoud and forget the national security my grandfather has hire and pay Armenian catholic lawyer 60000 usd to peace of heaven that is a great lifestyle.

Search serve protect

The real thing eutopia. For dia life chooses. Lebanon residency Saratoga spring veteran and military education school with international program Saratoga spring NY I enroll. Certify in Lebanon ministry of foreign affairs Pennsylvania accreditation amideast verify. BS in Business management economics with concentration in finance. 3.52 GPA. After graduation I had international surveillance communications that Lebanon ministry of foreign affairs base. There is also pro Lebanon bilateral agreement for university qualified approve by Lebanon become s approved by Armenia.

Sc and Syria

My aust student contract was affiliated to suny. Boutros Harb aust lawyer responsible. By Syria military Lebanon military with official suny and accordance of Lebanon executive body I am sent to standard Chartered the great Britain NATO together with HSBC for direct role in Vatican affairs pink floyd says walk on part in a war leading role in a cage is about the Vatican 2 formation under France Spain and Portugal as Russian blood start NY arms reduction continue as Syrian blood prepare to leave for second war like rf Lebanon the second Syria NY then third Turkey Italy. And sc is the main align woe that will be like satellite state in Syria NY USA I am the Lebanese Latin from Syria sent to bab idriss like saint maroun.

The day I go for suny entrance exam head of personnel loan warns pre explosion security risk of also pre know I leave I don't hear when reach aust student s tell there was bombing and I tell like Saddam Hussein knowing Hariri died issue ISIS.

Sc starts align wars with maronite skew faces secular laws the bombing Syria leaves and the second war.

Student assistant

By recommendation of ny I work 2 years student assistant at suny empire state pays 7 usd at hour during residencies and free assistance to students in between I assist half of the choosers to leave in 2006 to Turkey from Syria for the rest warship is sent then for 2 years after 2006 they don't come to Lebanon and residencies are done on the phone

2006 war with Israel

At standard Chartered were intervene for them hierarchy after I leave they continue 1 day at evening philange militia members open their automatic weapons saying Israel is attacking which enrages NY and within hours to next day Israel attackswi decide to go to Armenia Israel bombs the bridge in sharkieh I go 2 weeks 2 Armenia I receive from NY letter where did I go is the whole. I remember in 2006 cessation of hostilities Israel said in old we traded Cedars peaceful Lebanon responded now your doing war.

Suny Esc

While learning one of the benefit is ny active Israel air for ny defense me and Lebanon against maronite s. Which continue with secret cooperation with Lebanon government as degree haver by insider.

Graduate

Under difficult conditions I graduate the residency doesn't come because post 2006 and graduation is done at the affiliate by former USA ambassador officially there affiliate handed then shook hands with USA ambassador was the process.

Adult life

Ministry of foreign affairs and cultivation

Intelligence cultivation foreign ministry base that are influential people of world systemic.

Politics

Us ambassador prepare Lebanon politics and that time the word was is the prince.

Governor s Sara Palin and Carolina.

President Bush one of the most spend time with with code I want to be president of usa

Condoleeza rice who was Russian specific how could I defeat Georgia package I am responsible person in democratic government

Obamati was spending more time with Russian s I received not every foreign policy is nail to be removed.

Trump in Georgia rf against independence then like bush

Senator s policy base including Kennedy that was saying 2008 was not American Catholics was Zionist.

Vatican international Lebanon umbrella

Congressmen to war as I remember one of them was John Kerry

Corporate affairs

CNN security and money

Boeing aerospace business

Morgan Stanley central bank business

Oscars influence

Policy

Interventionism

On FBI Nazi intervention that have trump use nazi sign

May Flower   against standard Chartered and England intervention

Senators collapse Raffi and zionism

2 senator s dead intervention in Armenia

Jewish military personnel admittance of woes against USA state s and Adam Schiff from Congress in pain scream I'm sorry Raffi interventionism on Jews start in exclusive niche that Syria takes on the intervention and bombs gulan.

Israel

I know Netanyahu part of Lebanon Syria USA politics says to me this is who we are where do I stand regards interventionism raffi Lebanon small intelligence hizbullah khumeiniat with Armenia USSR Israel attacks phosphorus and Raffi hizbullah intelligence wars Lebanon dropping leaflets urging Lebanese not to leave their home.

Assassination attempts

Twice the Egyptian s try to kill me with standard Chartered for ancient Egypt reasons I use the alumni community and close to my policy in Egypt mine was only Egypt bring down their leader and put in path of defending Syria

Syria Civil war

The third Vatican war second continue war is inevitable USA is against Turkey and us damage in tcc is translated in creating ISIS and defeating like 1st continue maronite s in creating original indigenous continue for those bad societies in Lebanon the grip of peace there is no crime by Syria breaks in war and maronite s rule a second policy under ISIS in series of losing and in 2020 reach obedience the system is:

Loyal coming of hafez assad

Friendly 1990

Obedience 2020

Fallen bkerky under Turkey Civil war

Torture war by France against the Pope

Online alumni community

Veteran only Lebanon member

Criminal justice only Lebanon member

International alumni   only Lebanon member

Administration

Politics and business for Americans.

During Georgia war I was stopping support to Georgia during active war and succeed ends pro Russian I receive from Condoleezza rice how could I I am responsible person in a democratic government.

DIA DEF COM 5 DEF COM 2

Benefit a def com 5 money def com 2

Worthy of saying among many

In the last USA elections the section swings unfavorable Biden state to Biden leading his win against trump by my methodology state voted not the people according caucus and trump loved it and made statements using organization s more than a vote.

Rf and Lebanon interior ministry

Pregnancy and born

As Latin cilician s my parents go to Bulgaria to get the status Latin high cilician which outside the continent of Europe is a highest status but is orthodox background is second highest my grandmother is from orthodox background she said Ladin that is Latin for cilician s she would be allowed to marry European s outside the Latin section has marry an Armenian catholic thus that orthodox has family in English law Armenian catholic and thus as family the baptism belongs to orthodox has right of mating. The black don't have European rights and if baptism from Armenian catholic background is elysee Italian. Not da Italian if was not Latin. By crusade law is for second a few. Majority being Muslim. That is the blessing of the old continent.

Background and title

My father's mother is Latin sent from Syria to Lebanon for Europe and my mother comes from family relatives of House of lords and deputy governor of Lebanon central bank back then to be I was born in 1983 bouldoukian took the deputy governor position in 1985. I come from such background and in house of lords am the eldest grandson of arsho born after harout bouldoukian am father in House of lords.

Russian title to me

I am a high cilician who has taken the KGB am a child spy Bulgaria has gotten the Fatima.

Armenian orthodox

My children will also reign

Germany

The wife will be Germanic and I from Germany ministry of defense.

France

Macron to Germany Raffi will remain in the to the third Reich is Latin.

Lebanon civil war and rf

During the civil war the Russian s provided with aerospace systems for my safety and protection I remember star going on rogue Armenlan's and on rmeil philange party associated withme to going zahle.

Work and gain

- In Lebanon against maronite s: with aerospace attack on maronite s and after also with Chinese against maronite s the rf embassy security give s me the title mory.

- Armenia RF embassy regards Armenia: work detail security with rf embassy regards Armenia including have the Armenia security protecting the embassy hit for their believe.

- From special agent s Ully lg Ully rf passport

- Cold war against USA: I waged including manufacturing about 20 drivers manual cold war against USA where the driver s obey and the sky turn their suit colors.

- White Collar against USA under supervision of Putin I collaborated China rf alliance and EU rf alliance which USA was independently waring that brought end to the cold war.

- Rtr priest: USSR made me start priest according to my background.

- Rf inner circle to rf government the aerospace that is in collaboration with the Lebanon interior ministry created section together with Putin and rf ministry of defense inner circle to rf government.

- Psychological war: from early Biden second attempt as lost USA against rf a cold war mating with German s reduce announce cold war to psychological war.

Circles and status

Lebanon interior ministry and rf Lebanon embassy together with Bulgaria mingle with Putin and other senior rf leaders and with svr for co purposes and Russian benefit also Russian project from 2015 Putin has become a father figure cooperation individual ly and industries including the war industry and receive title slav king from industry support by Lavrov part of inner circle at rf government. Child spy is protected by Putin secret daughter. And 2021 security workers day Putin was at my agency praising me as a example.

PhD

From reaching certain development regards military the rf aerospace for PhD purposes issued 2 codes that means military protection thus

From rf military Beirut

I have PhD in

Military protection

Syria

Has Syria

When pregnant also got from Syria some people say I respect the last law of Syria the technical word is has Syria.

Hafez assad

I received for my defense title hafez assad for rigidity and non tolerance.

In / Damascus war s

My biggest honor is when in Damascus USA showed new found oil reserves the biggest in the world was Syrian s with Vatican judging.

I did Aramco in KSA it was deal with NY Iran target its USA relations

When received from USA Jewish intervention Syria took the cause and hit Golan.

Polite

My grandmother is Latin Syrian the Syrian s were polite to me.

NY

Inner circle to ny government

I am inner circle to my government that is I am secular loyal to their cause .

Ny gun

Rf provides aerospace gun ny gun is red fire.

Latin and Lebanese king

As Latin and Lebanese I have king status wher the rf was slav in nature.

Anti contrast (Zionist) ally to Donald Trump as cilician

As cilician I am invited to the anti contrast of Donald Trump I believe like Nasrallah of hizbullah the high cleric of Zionism that is making ny independent from USA like rfsf from USSR.

Hammer

Lebanon Lebanese hammer/ security is a Syria and Lebanon status for hierarchy of east where we have already waged war and came out victorious.

Jazaer Protect Christianity: Alger decided to be co loyal personal with me on this issue.

Libya co loyal Haftar : after the agreement Lebanon my strike brought Turkey and we participated with Azerbaijan against Armenia and won.

Sudan co loyal Sovereign: my section brought rf who is cooperate according nam Vatican.

Tunis protect dissolution: this is the agreement with Tunis

Ethiopia military loyalty USA: this is the agreement with Ethiopia is also cooperating ny Syria marriage.

Azerbaijan alliance Libya Sudan Hikmat: this is Azerbaijan Turkey Azerbaijan agreement with me with Libya my co militia s victorious.

Turkmenistan CIS Azerbaijan : is Azerbaijan in cis which with my assistance brought Turkey Azerbaijan Turkmenistan alliance co me.

Loyalty with Iraq part of Lebanon Iraq relation : here the agreement with both countries not me co personal.

Loyalty with Yemen part of Lebanon Yemen relation : here the agreement with the countries not me personal.

Alliance Nassrallah : there is Syria base protection alliance with elysee cooperation.

Alliance Hassan Diab : there is Lebanon base alliance

Jumblat alliance Future : there is Latin base alliance

Khumeiniat : haftar hizbullah intelligence co loyal that also did war with Israel.

Inner circle Lebanon : complete cooperation base on military implementation and Lebanon sovereignty and war against foreign and domestic enemies including maronite s.

Status at Exclusive Vatican : freemason base hierarchy cooperation and security.

Choice of gun and alliance s :

- From Beirut safe country personal France
- Elysee defends the Pope from France by melting limited
- National security king
- Vatican gun
- Security elysee
- Surveillance king
- Rf China ny Italy alliance

Politics

Finance and history also allegiance to Rome is comprehensive politics of mine 2 of my books that speak in detail other than this loyalty to rf imperialism to Zionism and to nazism.

China agreement : vatican base security agreement with China, fighting Hong Kong and personal House of lords legislation pass.

Italy : Mussolini base loyalty French loyalty and Italian loyalty from Vatican as boy not complete Italian including illicit furthermore detail specific fire gun from Italy.

Germany :

- War together with Angela Merkel against aligned
- Family nurture

- Nazism support including title Pope favorite person
- Pass a law nazism Ashraf rifi says child doesn't do this
- And interventionism on FBI regards nazi that France considers cheap and nasty

Social life

Agbu university student : i was member of agbu university student s and we debated issues and once we went weekend in the mountains faraway with disco was good.

Tekeyan head of scoutui ran the scouting efficiently we went to Syria for regional meeting is a good organization I sided with the Syrian s regards withdrawal from Lebanon Jordan said does with out Syria. And once we were invited to dinner at the center there was also parliamentarian Kassardjian.

Agbu sports committee is a sub committee we did meetings and taught chess I gifted 1000 usd worth of luxury charity program.

Freemason first with Druze and was guard then with maronite s sister of France ecclesia was also guard and was offered to work for money.

Miscellaneous works

Tbir: I work 2 years as tbir at Armenian orthodox church including go to school.

Nameless ido I got teacher beginner degree standard and Latin taught and went to nameless parties.

Librex I work outdoors Sales person.

Giro group: Data analyst I propose using financial ratios.

Saltek: accounting assistant I propose entering household ovens.

Parents

Background positive

Latin and millionaire cilician who is relative to House of lords and deputy governor of Lebanon central bank.

Background negative

My mother grandfather and his brother enemies and the families war brother wanted the factory there is division. My father and his brother catholic enemies war with government to harm each other there is division. I come from psychological bankrupt family. My uncle at 18 enter Lebanese forces militia hold gun did not tell the parents the sister study IT work at maronite bank at young age head skrewed.

Elie Frizli termed the lie family.

Trust fund

1 apartment in Beirut according to ivsc 1200 * 12 * 40 valuation 1 apartment in rabieh 1200 * 12 * 40 half apartment in Beirut 300 * 12 * 40 also business 2000 * 12 * 15. Comes about million and half dollars. My trust fund is about 200 from business and 100 from rent. There was a while were paying the whole amount now is deteriorated. To be Frank I am receiving 270000 lbp per month.

Background and Syria Civil war

Onig was killed for being Armenian years later maral tell s me story was going to die called the children cried on sissi fear from the rest and died. Guiragos brought wrong doctor, dirouhy maronite priest prayed felt pain and died in 2 days.

When Syria was in Lebanon there was no crime but after left the second war of continue sharkieh became little better than Lebanon Civil war and hratch and harout were owet fighters so were maral family.

Ed and Cairo

Manifestation and opportunity is a leading factor in 3 division s hratch harout maral. They are the 3 division s of from maronite s given national security.

Direction disagreements

 Is a blue collar and harout is right is he is saying what is right and I am not doing.

Fake and black hole

Was asking maronite s for more inside.

Harm wishes

Lower than maronite and physically changing like hijacking when the opportunity rose.

Changing luck

Self punishment and apology with manual hijacking.

Fake child

Loving other people sons and daughters.

The lie family Elie frizli

Murder attempts

Putting killing substances in juice. wrong doctor are the things have done.

Woe

Der mesrob

Farmer from Anjar my grandfather ousts guiragos says don't leave the fruits unattended the maronite steals goes and becomes priest fake friend sc has hit the telephone acts wrong priest to 21 years old I hear has deseases

Satellite providers and the cia

This people are the bottom less pit I told the CIA the street business of their divided to half.

Dr jiro

Fake friend puts me wrong in the deir salib with Russia I appease their salib the government prevents him to use relative mukhtar stamp.

National security on ordinary

Zack

Secondary school time friend changes to maronite circles marries maronite the surveillance when his working under the car the car moves and kills him.

Der oshagan

Removes the cross from my mouth regards character assassination then dies.

Armenian female neighbor

One time from the balcony saw her in her underwear died where she reached.

Second cousin ggrandfather

Told me I am like harout basmadjian my father died in a week.

Aunt father in law

Unhealthy people Lebanon took them

Aunt mother in law

Unhealthy people Lebanon took them

Cousin relative in law daughter

National security lies treason Lebanon took her

Nooritsa

There was no like that Raffi Syria killed her

Maroun khoury

Called me Palestinian and was senior maronite gun person treason to Lebanon rf aerospace kept him alive the hospital killed him.

Several fanfare qualify Khalil badawi Armenian Armenian church responsible s.

I work for the church princes who died by Lebanon.

Studio vatche

Sc research calls journalism for his wrong eye Lebanon kill

Government protections

Philange invasion

Under the aerospace for 2 weeks then I left for Armenia the maronite s invade over 2000 people get torture and killed and I die a few times am reputed.

Philange kidnapping

Coming from disco maronite s try to kidnap to torture and kill I call the rf embassy with their telephone flea.

Lf murder attempt

In bourj hammoud lf tries to kill mel the patrol the dog doesn't attack with its telephone and the maronite taking me to the dog hand gets broken from the rf aerospace.

Open fire

The cold war starts and USA opens fire on rf base of mine I die a lot become with out feeling pain jellyfish and rf succeed s.

Career

Sworn expert in finance at court

- National wars
- Specialize books
- Personal verdicts

Russian Spy

- World leadership

Hero the father

- National security wars

Bank of Beirut

I was taller less than year important was Armenia embassy was trying fraud from interstate bank on Morgan Stanley of trillion usd format stopped it while Deloite audit was sent watching and next of me standing.

Lord of the Wings

Accountant less than a year important is USA was going reserve on consuming its chicken I told owners the news and recommended opening in USA they were cooperating in Kirkuk with hotel with USA military at that time.

Owner

OBS&C

- Finance: privare equity/ soft currency/ hard currency/ digital currency/ banking products/ trading / central bank/ securities/ stimulus/ derivatives/ securitization.

- Business: alliance/ business/ outsourcing/ religion and culture/ OBS&C monster convention/ massive media: Raffi Basmadjian/ agro energy/ robomail.

- Ngo and government : fundraising/ tax collection s / OBS&C Aerospace/ OBS&C Space/ OBS&C Space Installation s.

The government gave official services:

- White religion
- Blue military

- Black finance
- Red monetary

OBS&C Armenia

- Regulated war factory
- Cigarettes accessories

Raffi Haroutiouni Basmadjian

- Large land development
- Regional country global presence
- Smart money

Armenia citizenship

Pre citizenship: with csto mainly force have appease maronite s and deir salib

Appease the maronite s and deir salib isf supported csto its csto and Lebanon that made my citizenship from Lebanon not ministry of diaspora.

The 6 years

Till prison was good I enjoyed I have on the ground power. Armavir is a sick place and I don't take Armenia citizenship is the whole.

Csto

Incorporate from Vatican stronger than NATO but not Vatican NATO from divide you helped me from China I care .

Relation

Azerbaijan is the relation I am Frank for goodness black s with you is the Vatican no relation.

Woes

Closing citizenship

Lebanon court said I am deprive so me in Armavir is illegal. I did pashinyan and manukyan with USA and pashinyan did the elections and resign. Was the first friendly move no relation.

Lebanon (remaining)

- Sheikh
- House cilicia in antakia
- Fryer
- Religion

Davos the leadership sided with my direction and Trump became a role model.

Basel I independently and with Bemo Bank went to Basel with OBS&C speculation risk and close is manufactured.

Wars wage and status

Pierre gmeyel

Ny said to aust to kill boutros harb is the lawyer did it aust small organization.

Nahr bared general

Tashnag with muslims did it because open on me rays.

Sfeir

Ny with Vatican and Lebanon took out the position and rf aerospace killed him died with smile.

Standard Chartered

I with expert and with Lebanon military closed in Lebanon rf and me reduce the stock from 1700 usd to 350 usd.

Nubarashen

Ny Lebanon and Azerbaijan the war ended when holiday spring in China which is part of Soviet China together. Lebanon did the covid to counter the align threat. While I was there cilicia and ny did from ny sahagyan (which was done by us) doctor speaker of the house and removing Abrahamyan completely .

Port of Beirut

Was Lebanon military to have part of maronite religious like aoun and philange became like aoun.

Jean obeid

UAE ny and Lebanon did outside Vatican intervention and was over with bkerki international conference that admitted maronite defeat.

Egypt

NY and Lebanon for align Israel including murder attempts to me.

Israel

Prosecuton of natanyahu and bebe also multiple Knesset dissolution and USA and rf security consultations.

Psychological war

Germany ministry of defense to non character move.

On going Lebanon president

Syria did the civil state which reached bi cameral promise but in Syria Civil war end will happen smaller Taef. Aoun said going to hell this time is executive body Hariri handling big. I suggested shift from president to prime minister rule.

Auxiliary

Pakistan

Ny my lawyer s strategy for sc purposes direct.

USA

Cold war defeat well discuss in this book we lost Bush father and McCain to treason.

USSR

Align chose face destroy I say from 15 12 apostles it was non apostles republic s and one night on Egypt channel Nune Yessayan sang dle yaman in ancient Egypt language.

England

Ties with Vatican standard Chartered Brexit is not me is bigger though is the from western Europe EU the next step we war honk Kong and thank House of lords for legislation the intervention on England was ny was us.

Status

Suny empire state

Alumni employee and community member in Georgia we chose the Russian military that concludes works as veteran and Condoleezza rice is right I say sadest thing I experienced ever value base work.

Sworn expert in finance at court

I thank the court for showing me Lebanon is a best country. Truth base.

Hero the father

The tile or assigning is new but is been with me the whole time cooperate with Russian s . Maronite s are passing Lebanon laws a Description.

Child spy

A most cherished part of me you and Latin both is my ruski my small and big.

Lebanon court

From childhood doing his job I thank is the bible holy spirit.

Syria

I am non Syrian mother law does Lebanon is Syria start.

Turkey and Elysee

When the divide militia s from upper intermediate are created you were there for me like Syria was in Lebanon.

Elysee is my fairytale and bigger home.

Lebanon Syria Turkey

Lebanon Syria Turkey are 3 non white s will have indeginous east not France in Vatican 2.

Lebanon and center

Treason

In middle of war der ghevont lochkadjian with my family including harming Lebanon diplomacy hijacks and puts me in sanitarium it was the second attempt first at Armenian sanitarium in 2013 as another treason but fail pashinyan being come more than Lebanon embassy was Indiana parliamentarian the bilateral work gets damaged and Bush senior and Vatican umbrella McCain get murdered Lebanon with Iran win by force and trump in France is wary of assassination this is high treason against Lebanon.

Lebanon rescue plan

In 6 months time Lebanon military attacks Palestinian camps aoun says return to Palestine Palestinian saied does meeting with Nasrallah during this time Lebanon sends municipal police to the hospital ministry of health and minister close and put the Palestinian in prison my father last day of fanar says I will rotten and die in fanar. Mimosa from family gets charged prison also and the government steals harout car. While I am in fanar semi gmeyel goes rf and says what we all die.

Life at the center

Ministry of health brings me back to sharkieh and puts me not in a hospital but a center where I continue working and the center under treason loses brother of owner day time security and 2 batch of Syria replacement s. I have no medicine from ministry of health only bed that is tied to Lebanon hanging machine.

2020 2021 part 1

Is the time where Syria war ends network hack happen and Vatican gave gun to trump who did the Capitol riots. And maronite obedience start official ly.

CV

Raffi Basmadjian

Usa.raffi83@yahoo.com

Mobile 81 340461

Mission statement

To get finance / history qualified position at your esteem university

Qualified

Sworn expert in finance at court

Obsandc.webstarts.com

Obsandc-gddh-trading.webstarts.com

Obsandc-Armenia.webstarts.com

Rhbads.webstarts.com

Lcmwatani.webstarts.com

M-t-l.webstarts.com

Lebanonfranciscanreligion.webstarts.com

Erme.webstarts.com

Englishroyal.webstarts.com

Childspy.webstarts.com

LLH.WEBSTARTS.COM

Rafficlub.webstarts.com

Saied-raffi.webstarts.com

Raffisyria.webstarts.com

Suny esc bs in business economics management with concentration in finance

Experience

- Closed sc in Lebanon
- Fought against USSR
- Solutions regarding the revolution and crisis
- Experience in English Catholisis
- About anti Mason party and trump declaring obsolete NATO
- Iran Syria Lebanon with Arab league regarding Israel and USA
- Break even maronite s

Moral of the story

When I was learning humanities I studied why a person dies at young age and the person went to China to find out God takes near him. Well from capuchin I come as Latin saint and reply no half Christian full Christian.

Preview part 2 road and Unrest Raffi Basmadjian autobiography

As a man I choose my path I choose that Lebanon already started protecting Turkey for 3rd continue war religion and then Syria will protect France under closure where is against Pope and Turkey will not protect this research of mine is my heroes I follow his road. This is the next 60 years.

OBS&C aerospace program with Lebanon

The light is gun is act of God frequent.

الرئيس الأول لمحكمة إستئناف بيروت

محضر تحليف اليمين القانونية المنصوص عنها في نظام الخبـراء

للخبير السيد باصمجيان رافي هاروتيون

نحن : القاضي جان فهد

الرئيس الأول لمحكمة إستئناف بيروت

وبحضور كاتب الضبط السيد عمـاد فرشوخ

مثل أمامنا، في يوم: الثلاثاء الواقع في: ١ / ٢ / ٢٠١١

الخبير السيد : باصمجيان رافي هاروتيون

رقـــم : - ٢ - الجريدة الرسمية العدد ٥ تاريخ ٢٠١١ / ١ /٢٩

الفـرع : الشؤون المالية.

المحافظـة : بيروت.

وحلف اليمين القانونية المنصوص عنها في المادة ٣٠ من المرسـوم الإشتراعي رقم ٦٥ تاريخ ٩ / ٩ / ١٩٨٣.

جرى تنظيم هذا المحضر على ثلاث نسخ، إحداها في قلم المحكمة، وسلمت الثانية الى الخبير، وأرسلت الثالثة الى دائرة الخبراء في وزارة العدل لوضعها في ملف الخبير الشخصي.

في

الكاتب
عمـاد فرشوخ

الرئيس الأول لمحكمة إستئناف بيروت
القاضي جان داود فهد